DENDRITE
BALCONIES

DENDRITE BALCONIES

SEAN BRAUNE

Brave & Brilliant Series

ISSN 2371-7238 (Print) ISSN 2371-7246 (Online)

University of Calgary Press
2500 University Drive NW
Calgary, Alberta
Canada T2N 1N4
press.ucalgary.ca

LIBRARY AND ARCHIVES CANADA CATALOGUING IN PUBLICATION

Title: Dendrite balconies / Sean Braune.
Names: Braune, Sean, 1985- author.
Series: Brave & brilliant series ; no. 10.
Description: Series statement: Brave & brilliant series, ISSN 2371-7238 ; 10 | Poems.
Identifiers: Canadiana (print) 20190137169 | Canadiana (ebook) 20190137207 | ISBN
   9781773850955 (softcover) | ISBN 9781773850962 (PDF) | ISBN 9781773850979
   (EPUB) | ISBN 9781773850986 (Kindle)
Classification: LCC PS8603.R3835 D46 2019 | DDC C811/.6—dc23

The University of Calgary Press acknowledges the support of the Government of Alberta through the Alberta Media Fund for our publications. We acknowledge the financial support of the Government of Canada. We acknowledge the financial support of the Canada Council for the Arts for our publishing program.

Printed and bound in Canada by Marquis
♻ This book is printed on Lynx Opaque Ultra Smooth Cream paper

Editing by Helen Hajnoczky
Cover image: J.U. Lloyd and C.G. Lloyd's *Drugs and Medicines of North America*.
   Cincinnati: Press of Robert Clarke & Co., 1884, plate XXIII.
Cover design, page design, and typesetting by Melina Cusano

CONTENTS

lapsus declivity
wet ribs project

      heresy—
      a ciborium lies open,
      convex concavity

            in tableaux hands. tired.
            all is a damn misery—
            numb
            and infernal.

<strings>
        <tie things>

      i'm voltage.

FACIALITY

1.

foliated skin
water on water
    pride-full, fluid depth.

classify devils,
climb high fire scales
    and cry out, as outages
        kneel in the cirrus.

triumph, my little jesus,
    plants the *you*
in *you*, fashion
        the rain circus, cue
           jésus la caille.

cadences are material,
    random paradises of
indignity, of choler, they are
    the salt wedge speckling
        childhood anger.

in lockstep
    by the locked door,
a cadenza of stanzas
        permeates your
put-on bravado
    jeune homme.

sulphate now,
    later is painful,
        plentiful.

immunity, reluctant to time
    questions like lemon tissue:
"bathe my sea wings."

phantom maneuvers,
    a crack in a limb like
a code or line on a map,
        struggling—an agon.

rolling a cigarette
    after dinner, clutching
        onto summer,
"eyes drink the soul of winos."
"summer love," when I clench
        your face in a smush

2.

angular cough
sardonic satan

the portrait swallows faciality
the gallow keys are subtleties
the reader police

are authors that arrest, redefining
product boycotts.

translate the exposure of
gestures, all agog, moss is
your trespass.

trepan, the revulsion,
the homicide television
revises sayings:

"my photocopies
are money."

please bankroll delirium.

3.

terror vacant as a
butterfly's weak whisper
at a spy wasp.

spas specialize
in hornet caches—
in plurality.

a hidden catch of
shark's teeth, shucked,
mouth "bisphenol a"

tucked into a smile as
you writhe—my
smug guppy.

4.

irreverse the conduit of your throat,
wipe the flighty inverse skirmishes
from you, obdurate and faceless.

the sample of tumult
is two lips, is an appropriate exposé.

turn up the

>*hot hot hot*
>and derive pleasure
>from the turn please
>and re-turn
>and de-turn

a bird is spillage, is plumage and
lists, is sill, and still, and silts
at the borderlands,

>ganache lists
>for sugar feet.

you half-ass the armageddon
now cleared of jeggings, of kryptonite.
the retweet of i am. i am
a zoroaster or zero-star, a horrorshow, a zombie.

a tan line story, a tea slop,
a partial periphery totes
the uncanny valley of our
skype-date.

we vape and recall
yarn-bombed ghosts,
the door is
in exile, now
dead.

i seeded emptiness to density to
assume a silence that flickers
in nighttime equations.

equipoise all equality or
the fragrant carcass of
transcendence. open the instant
roads and encounter
the clamor of a spindle
smashed in the rhythm of its
intensity.

        emit warmth in this
        clear cold lucidity.

certainty persists time's
broken feathers,
line-by-line,
disciplined in crasis,
language's static
stratified, line-by-line, composed
and curled by each night.

i bless this porosity
the cipher police
the siphon
her cyclone
is a lion, is a lone,
all one and ecstatic
like a loner

        we circle the outtakes
        baked in the bay
        garish and sanguineous

my seraphim,
my sinus ache
revived, drifting in redux
nail me to the driftwood
and let me float in memory

in mercury
like the neon needle
found in the arm
of wakening.

5.

incendiary harmonies immolate
the pastor's sleep. yawn, the yearly,
forge decades, yearn for
the majesty of the sea, you son of helios,
this music

infected signals
invisible touches

obsidian bonds, obsequious,
constellate the pain that follows
the flow downward

ravel the raven's trammel,
the oceanic ebb of what follows.

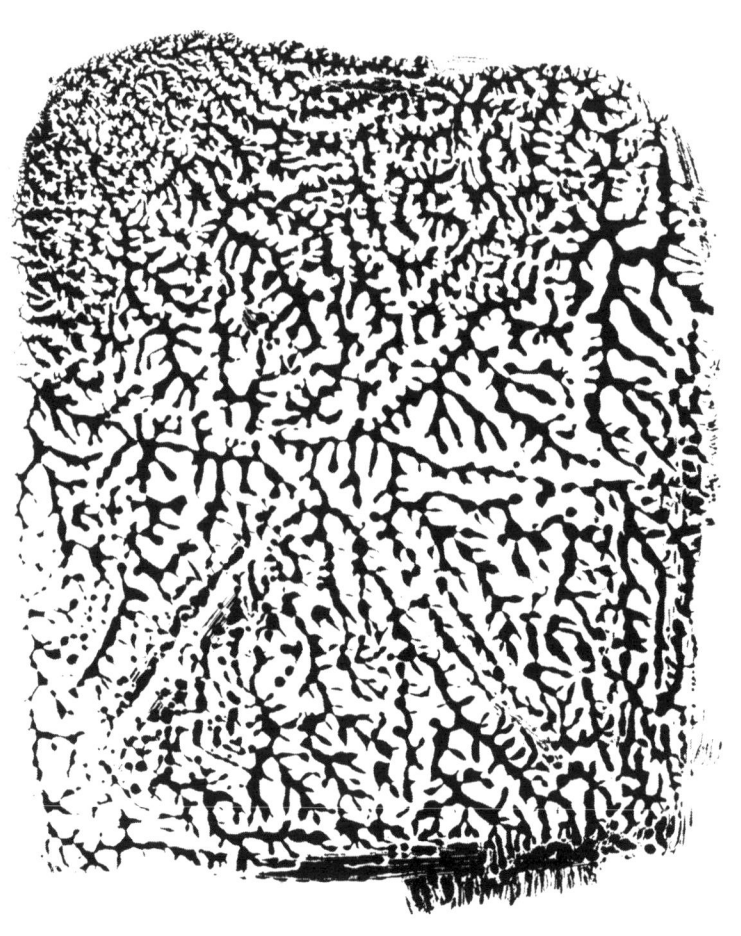

CHIASMUS PLANET

1.

neither a smile's similitude, nor the kraken's
coarse sand sister—no one weathers her

textured watch, glass-filled dresses,
degenerate folds, a song of glyphs,

her density is a ballad,
a ball, a pallor of hands

schlick feinsand turns sapphires to ash, to
feral knots bled gold with chaos

inspired limpets descend through the black,
through the happenstance of atoms.

three eyes today hiss jagged knowledge
in distemper, disrepair.

unload the shadows,
denude the crystals.

heresiarch bellows.

2.

with *my blizzard ecology*
i tickle their gaze,
gathering in their wrongs
that say:

> "I want to lunch
> w/ work mottos."
> regular and modular,
> not a theatre speaks,
> nor a machine.

knot/form
wave/form

daily fatalities, acute as spines,
as the flicker and morphs of gemstones.

alien nationalism
    overtakes the traffic's moan.
      "soluble globule,"
        we whispered under the stars.
our current, durational richness.

memorial defects, the whale bone song
sings horribly

the bandwidth of planets
serpentine prowling

words spill
as they merge

with the slosh from
this recently

synthetic
you

3.

lazarus cesarean,
a handful of furls.
unfair oxen and
the lynx god.

the morning begets
the burning
the wallow
or this wonder
from the marginally
bare.

your body's words
act like a corset that was
a corsage on the roadway.
"stitch me," my subject,

       moi

nervousness is in
my hands,
a quorum of essence

       "exquisite pronoun"
       she whispers to me
       her flesh coral,
       here, growth
       arises, corpselike
tongue the naught

the night's coil
slither, lit, her.

    the scroll
    the reveler
    its liberty
    bowie knife
    cut-up foliage

        thou tablet betides
        each alphabet's roulette.

        gunshot,
        smoke.

        vowel down.

the day shimmers

4.

this kiss spoons
all crystal clairvoyance.

light spears
aspirate grand angles.

solstice spires
"sweetly embrace"

                breath.

invasions recorded in braille,
a hornet's garden composed
like a sentence.

acanthus candle
flickering in the breeze
of a dendrite balcony.

all is cybernetic.

        willow-green
        archaeological caricatures
        remark that

downfalls balance colours
        as   vowels
        or   awls,
owls blink like struck wolves.

textually indistinct intensity,
now bloodily arborescent.
gravity itself is virtual.
perimeter blur, filaments
or drift in eyelash saccades.

succor
—the dynamism that
speaks each word.
word-by-word
micropattern panels
the mutable strangeness of
the control panel.

their progress is word-by-word,
like the extended lattice of taproot.
we walk in tandem, swallow attrition,
then flatten the primal scene.

       the *schauplatz* dancers
       refuse their vertical carrion
       "control the branch
       "control the chaos
       "control the lungs

our muscles contort our black cells:

       a cradle of
       the filthy water will
       slake our tired throats.

5.

bones   ex   pand
as successive mosaics deflate
flattened and gut choral
the thunder is   everyone else's
sunshine pollinating her chevrolet.
the daring ghost who mulched paper:

> *here i am overdrinking*
> strategically in the white grid.
> *we should all start feeding,*
> lachrymose and frozen.

two humans on a park bench
pulling feathers from their hair
posed like a frieze at the moment
of puling viscosity.

> half-moon is the sole
> window frame of the
> parking lot.

inhale the downward stars,
en-garden.

these dead systems,
walkways.

> climb the stairs
> to the podium,
>
> the end of days.

6.

temptation tickles crystal
as vanity acquires words.

       arise, in this chamber,
       the swelling demon.

archive palimpsests

       male
       female
       e-mail

starlight philosophers
            walk for hours,
            we are forgetful things—
            an objectal shell-house,

                  blood-filled
                  with virtue.
                  reluctantly, he

smears the eternal poison
on the jugular writ

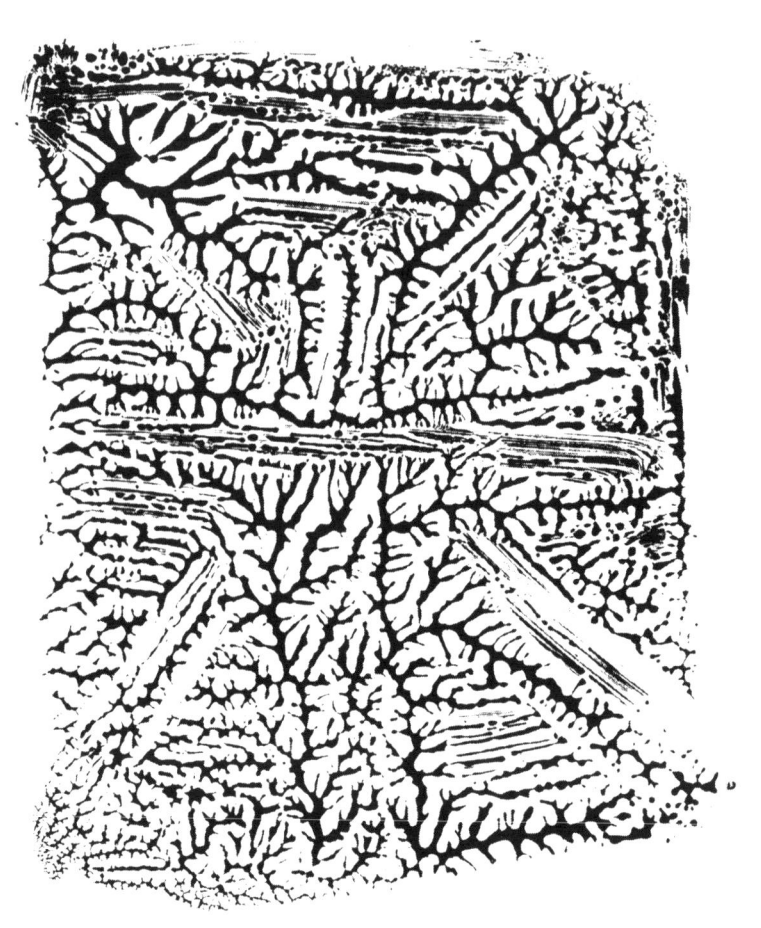

THE UNMIXED SKIN VOID

1.

within autobiographies
   faculties approach
indecent reliquaries
hold lively registers
open counsels in integral rooms,

          but the spiral
          integers of *palindromes*
like the spoken nothings that
remain of her assured portraiture.
my paper flower grown in colonnades,
thickets of egos encased in snowdrifts
like forgotten lovers.

the dusting of snow crystals
a cribbed desert
swaddles imagination

shredded, fontanelle,
          its oceanic weeping.

the fluorescent warmth, the nightmarish
finality of text, connecting and
collisions, virulent and

the city perches, impossibly bare,
encrusted in ice, sacrilegious
snowy lives speak in
jagged cuneiform:

your deictic pressure buckles.

hear

the disappearance is deathly.

2.

corrupt sand,
iridescent
petropolitic eye tics blink like
fireflies like the windows of
towers at night, like the glint of
the bootleg military marching to
futures that bleed into the
harmony of the present

moment, the moment reveals
      she sees the
      of the he that
      sees the they
      of the them

or the whole of the all the nearly
and almost quiet or ruddy sand or
the flowers, wholesale gamble but a
brushstroke, orange the quake, a
follicle that touches another of the
they that is of the quiet solitary one

I see
stumbling along
the street.

a stripling planet bent on a plane
or a comet's tail that looks through the
epoch's mirror, or the gravel plasma,
the blood pumps towards

breathing in the stale or the chill
that calls us, that
finds us, children of an age
　　　without
　　　birth, without
　　　cold,

only the caress of follicles, or
a murmur of unknowing skin
against our own

unknowing skin, that sensation,
across a void, that feeling
interwoven with technology
　　　itself across a void, all touch is now "ouch."

3.

each glance a timbre of
sensations feel around the
ceiling our lofted resolutions

holding up memory's wounds,
echoes of my dear's exploits,
vaulted ash, the wound

exists like an ice crust over
water that no longer lingers,
casting a shadow that emits

impressions told by a finger
pressed into and melting the
nouns, their magic

4.

tonic crumbles, ethics salient
the grimy men, axe-hum, a
sense of dignity. unveil

each tire, but the lilac
after luster fades in the bedrock,
asleep as mulch clears

the fatal flaunting, the dust.

time is adamant.

our caress
bespeaks.

5.

our brined eyes blink epistles
and streets, weeping in
libraries, coins are eyes

or debt that skims our
tidal lips. a wilt
at daybreak,

but daylong shocks of numbness
close hope of memory as rome's
conspiracy dishevels the garments

all babel, tears,
and fugues struck
figural, as always.

aeries sway
to the cyclone's
one-eyed terror.

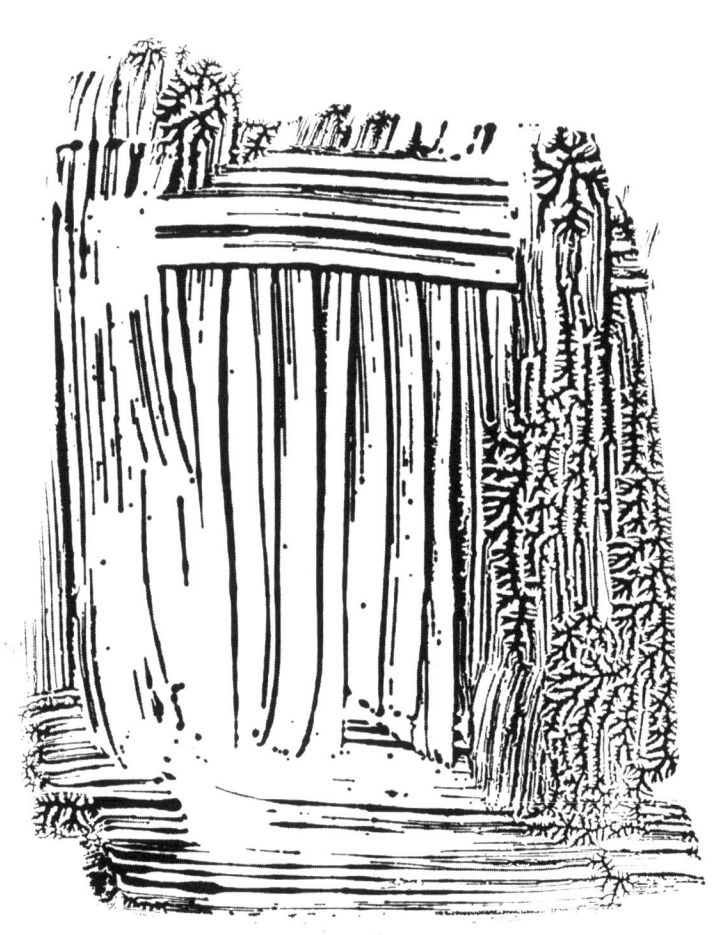

WATER DREAMS

1.

fortunate wisdom, writ in priestly
scribbles, radiated signatures
in prose.
succinctly buzz

in the telegraphy, fire it,
stiff and now the clang,
awake and auras ignore her

laughter. speak in gestural
circles, race the radii to the
secrets, curious. a prodding

in my dreams of water,
all full and corpulent.

2.

grip the roadside, its angular harvest.
the republic crawls towards the shelter.

drop rhetorical lineage, your avid
vocal business is as tea is capricious,

deleterious, skies emit delirium,
but decorous scuffling tapers imbricate

in the distance. muffler smoke and
carnage, a capacity to forage an owl's

oral greed.

3.

personae are slippery streams.
spheres are studded
with tragedy.

      a clear ring of existence
      is a sound that rings until
the void or the resilience
of the few flawed resonate

      high atop the overflowing
      hourglass, with its ennobled gains.

you, the blanket of ink.

4.

think deviation of the register relegated off the
switch trapped in the is of the class act

my sister is a leaf blotter like my friends were
rave queens. drag me to the sand spur

or in the wheels of a drag race, but in this
age what has long hair become.

a plant of peopling unvoiced. any political
poem must first consider the flesh of

the people now so suffused with the bait
and switch of the sin, but sin is only missing

a *k* the way shoppers hanker for a product
suction cup or when *the a* pins the alley cat.

There is no one left and no better venue.
apparently, we are near tears. a lizard's

scar, a tirade, a warm slough after the day's
hard drive. *that is contemporary depression.*

or has depression changed. The heat wave
destabilizes the engine in the laboratory of

drying geraniums, raw causation, gerunds,
and chipped teeth.

phoneme
money
tone
honesty
zone

nonce
dunce

5.

words feel,
words meander,
words glacial know words
in word dilation,
pupil-words
study temporalities, forget word
loss, press against word
knowledge, shadow, traditional
harmonies summarize icy voices
loudly. atop the barricade, words
responsibly, linguistic permanence,
surveyed by word silence, deliver
melancholy. crowds, margins,
acoustic word style,
independence surrounds
t(r)ails, regions of
unknowing
calumny
cloudy

6.

you fated happy character, all is
altitude, all is solitude. location origins,
percussion grenades, evaporate
like the steam off a viscous pot of
swan soup, growth organs boiling,
the first line of dialogue: "i drank
three swamp kisses," then violent
hands balustrade appearances.

a distant revelation, a lonely legato
grammar, dusk envelops platforms,
halos faintly glow in the gloam.
a bound manor. organize and prowl
spaces measured in duration like a
haunted bookstore. canonical then
incandesce all recalcitrant follies
are relinquished as our indulgences
arrive on displays that betray
our inability, our longing.

now autumnal, o noble cicada,
publish the wing shutters, the palace
dreams, drown in the burning stalks,
incruent, gambreled forevers, now
callously "mkay," our rage is now as
it was, quiet.

heroically. irascible.
autotuned backronyms,
deistic objects of shaded
painters. a birdhouse lights the galleria,
illuminating manuscripts of pokeweed
bound in pinchbeck, their neolithic folly
of pseudomorphs, so crass and full of
ugly scribbles. "what is the pageview,"
you ask. your spasm, your photobomb.
dust mites beaten with truncheon batons.

sunmotes rain trunnions, sunnily
demolish vector futures, humanity's
overheat staycation. stick to dartboards
and smuggle heroic awesomesauce,
await the sloth, for we are all hangry.

recall that shangri-la clocks nothingness,
sticky and insipid, this viscid memory.

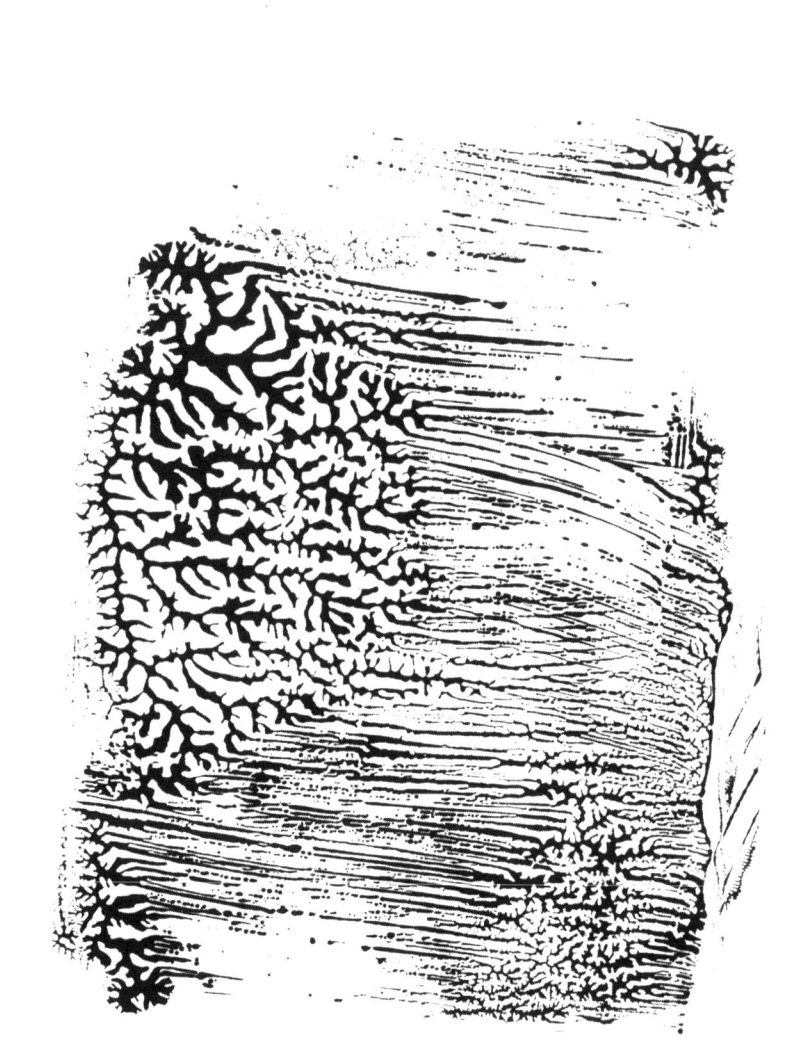

A CORPUS EMPTINESS

1.

the surety of daylight bathes the burnt
doctor in a cupreous lustre, a stimulant to
endure. the amethyst hour, unequivocally
imagist, the manspreading collective
crowdfunds the kidnapping. we require hair laughter to
appeal to one and all.

    i have fingers in the dying sky
    as if i glossed below the groaning pulp.
    i guide the moans towards
    the shattered ghosts,
    the machine-gun smile of last June.
    a wolf martyr, burnt free from
    the metaphor's coal mirror, its frost.

    i teethe the shadows, the cellular
    borders of the self that i fumble with
    in shambles. my self, fearfully anticipated,
    my self earned or morose, my self flies
    in search of jelly notes, then my soul sings the dreams
    of infected trees.

i dawdle between two minds.
i tie the border with a sash.
an eye spill, *idem.*

2.

mutant figures' civil emergence
shells seances in this habit
tread the light-path

subject to readerly rudders
i am trapped in a dull chase
to the epitome or your plenty
of lilies, an enemy with
noisy riches exists at love's pull as a
rapid pulse urges the
dumbest trifles to stick

>   our organs yield dreams
>   or publicity, a prick in the
>   spleen means fatherhood

>   *the amber, a ruckus,*
>   *a corpus of emptiness.*

rustic mysteries wander freely,
our laugh is the finely tuned patter
of fluke skeletons.

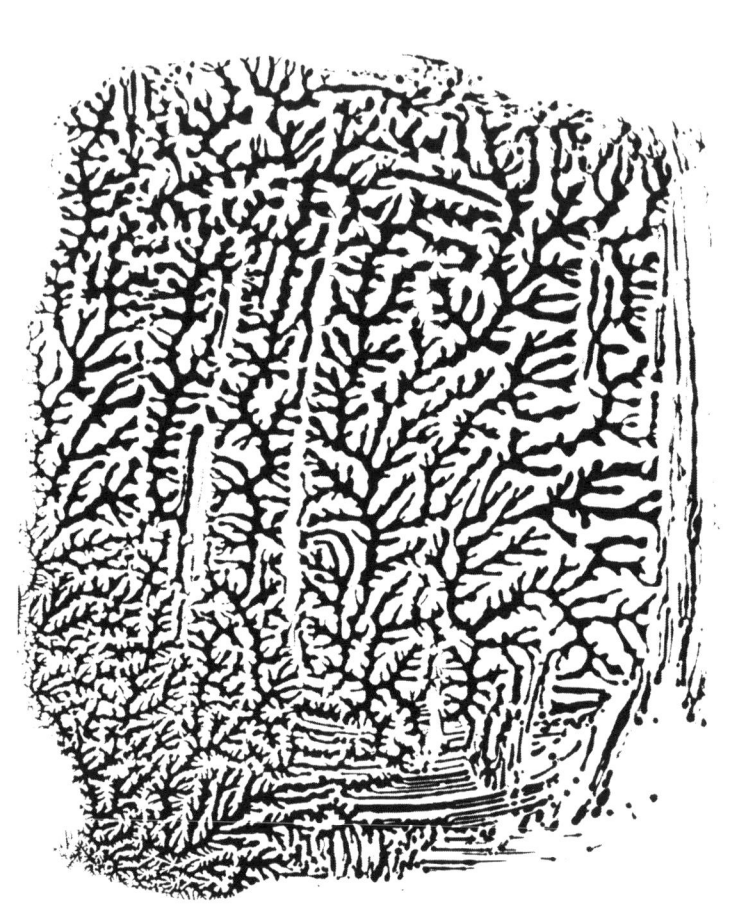

VITALOGISTICS

1.

an envelop of emptiness,
a nest of waste.
grope and blend hilarity.

> i thought the blindness was
> your exposé. sorry, i mean,
> marry me, expose every hallmark

or the holiday mirror with your breath.
the abyss looks and i like its figment,

> perhaps one can   gleam the fruit.

flowers tended by arrogant gods,
we slash it and
paint monsters.

2.

her father eats good meats
and chicken fat.
      "what are you,
      a lilac?"

he said he would be
home for dinner, but he
lied to you about that.

nearby the bed at midnight
and midnight is the time that
holds pieces of a beard.
      her eyes are now wrinkled stars
      and that is acerbic and a saying
      that is sometimes said when

i visit the continent.

3.

a crooked potlid.
your tomcat is unlocked, "please
steady before the rouge hits the wave."

you are humourous, officious.
our blood is consanguineous
and thinning.

a thing shifts by the mattress.

the languor broods against
rowing brows of memory.

      a blind memory.
      a blind arrow.
      a periphery of quiescence

or could moreover. another arrow
of time, the "e" hurries.
gallic testaments,
sung as
      you swim.

for longing tastes of tidal longitude,
my wit's ascorbic acid,
      my poetics wilted, "kid."
your hair looks
      like a green, leafy vegetable
or the vitamins
      of an alphabet.

4.

Vitality is the river that balances the shadow children.
Trust finds another *fini*, finally.

The world is doors.
piling language.

My grapheme is a grab-bag for a haemophiliac
in oneiric states of *aire.*
   An effete star.
   An onion made to peel.
A union breathes.
   Athens is a city that lives
   Hermetic rivers,
   filled with owls.

A paw or the
   howitzer's grimace.

The grimy whole opinions are cherubs when *pi*
designates the mathematical point at which
input designs
   thematic *Ich*s
     await insulation.

De sign the author's signature. A signature is a list
of ligatures, but with cursive allusions when curses; i.e.,

natures of sig—index all auras of alluvial air—
my song of terror

melts you.

       Sin is in us.

                 Eat.

                 Chew.

                 Swallow molasses.

5.

exordium,
the aleph equation, an
alphabetic terrarium. touch the letters
and caress the cursive's ligatures as
libations, tying letters to train track tables.

the letters exist in phonemic sounds
       transfer energies into stratified states,
       static.

do letters live,
do they exist beyond this typing,
or are they only the entities
that pile up in my speaking that seeks
the meaning of a tiled dream, tilting

       a lattice work effects
       no nourishment because a cause is a use
       of being a caucus of tic tac toe cacti
       casus belli.

the moon's arm-twisting rises
a dandy specter. an eye is a ye "e" postulate
of possibly, now late.

       I drink heterocyclics as my foe
       spills addresses. pills bilious,
       language trips on the doorstep.

words rip like a sword, like a miracle.
reality is eaten while lighting
           the number ten's nonsense
              that numbness is.

Language hiccups, but language
has a body where that body is here.

"w" of the seduction that says
what is said, said aids an "s" to
find an "a" at the he with a
"t" here in an "e" where an at is.

languorous, gauge. the auger
shows the "y," which itches
like a german *ich*

       minus the haitch.
       said in a hat belonging to "t,"
       but all the while "t" longs for the
       "h."

so "ha" says the i, giggling with
"w" smugness.

6.

now, ow,
      no. proem.

poem trees
      are not palm trees
      which is not
         a pomme tree.

    taste
      apples
         pulsing.

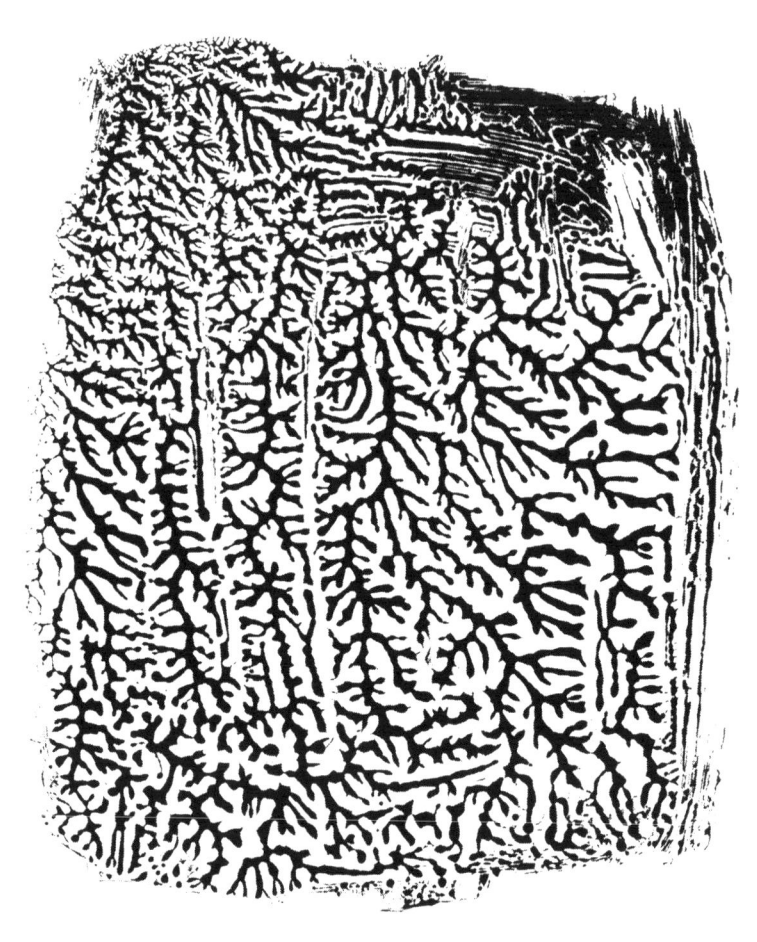

AN ORGAN DANCER

1.

the easy etiquette of a shy demon.
a stone, a step, built on a step to
a banquet.

progress to the morning, deathly
gallerias of dead stones are egos
with eye wings, stoppered,
needlessly dead.

new knell, she says. my next book
will be called "witness," *then churn*
truckloads of sawdust. life's
a damp churn. we have cultures
and damp muscles.

build sinuous tendons to tenuous
temperance, recall sinews respire
this blanket-hole sunday, recline
to balance the new in vain.

i see your abdomen
balance razorblades.

a wet room geography or the
exhaustion of processual
darkening.

consolidate criminality—
it's everywhere today.

lightly rot the gall and the
wasted fortune.

perspective crime, social
constructs, the churn and
settle of our roiling stomach
afternoons.

bury the residue in the boxcar.
hide the misplacement of silent
burglaries. these are our
strategic roles. i have one hundred
apologies on this, the loveliest night.

you paint your thighs with a crackle.

the patron is an organ dancer,
a dead ship. a new political system.
a data point in a database.

a mortuary, a revel, a borderline.

death is entrenched in cellular
sheaths, eroding the quiet.

we are visibly lascivious, we are
drenched in lacquer, we are the
song of the lost.
we are florid dreams, tonalities
and entropy, we inspire subtlety.

>uneasy wind,
>alter this gall.
>the sails,
>the tourniquet
>that binds
>the burden

these hurricanes, your words.

2.

it is here that everything is known
and heard and understood with the
utmost clarity

the length and sale of
affections begets the dripping dead god
hidden in the furrows of your address.

my sky is autumn and stifled as a dance.

purify the collapse. doze and inure
rubble to a dozen forms of purity,
you reprehensible gutter rat.

the callous darkness and then today's arrival, further
exhaustion. *thanks for the journey.*

trees correct earthlings. the public fog.
all idolatry. a cloud competes. libraries
upload drug wars, hybridity, and the anxieties

of corruptive birds.

when you heard astronomy was the
bedroom symptom, a wave broke
disorderly and negative.

        awkwardness,
        rickets,
        kisses, hisses,

veins estimate the exit.
red curtains rain to negotiate depression.
my attentional perplexity

        covers the dance hall
        blood matrix. *never forget*
        my soul weighs

the same as black magic.

3.

Abandon tepidity. "Life is a trough."

Bring up the last thought bubble
With frail lungs scratched in
tubercular schisms.

The visitors eat junipers.

their slimy purpose, all erratic objects,
        the dirt is all with few exceptions:
        a prophet's
        beautiful emanations.

I laminate emotions for fun when layers
blend to infinity, when layers recede.

Scenic fabric, a squabble, a vessel
redeems my peripheral demons.

I square off the circumference.
We quarrel. Part and then
overthrow beacons:
       "I think this idea is a constellation
       of another fable's catacomb."

"I hear danger"
overheard in the attic
Continue until the insurrection arrives.

Only *perplexity, rigidity, and complexity*—
newly accurate subjects.

Fornicate erasure and construct moonlight
at the children's ladder. An apple,
an aplomb. Speech erases joy in the
prison-house of pleasure.

necrology is only prettiness
all cleaned up.

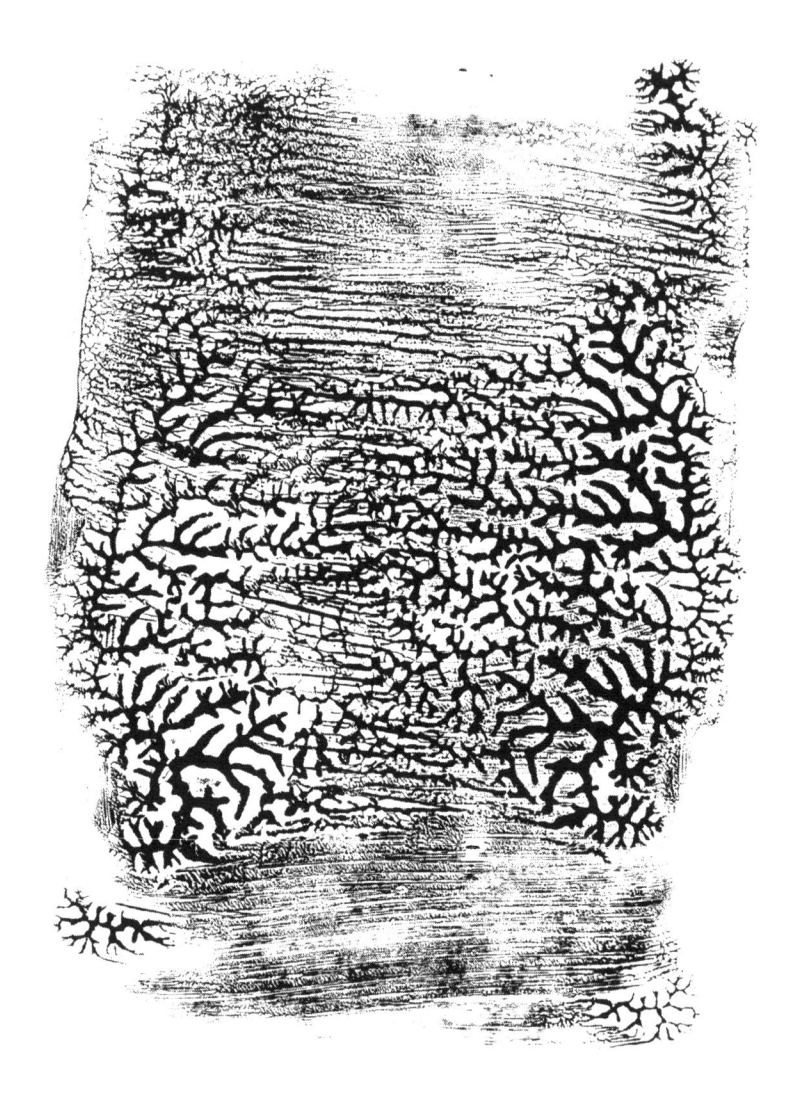

A WET ROOM GEOGRAPHY

1.

genres hum goodbyes,
transcribing deities
without truth, but
with geography.

epistolary tactics inhabit
the territory beneath
the continent.

another inverse nest
immolates memory.

strategies like sleeves
dipped in the acidic failure
of the past, paltry civilian.

the typewriter purge
accompanied the raining
floor, a wedded affair of
maps and returns, such
contributions.

      ceremonial
      colour and shelter

collapse.

his numinal anima is bright
like a valuable object.
the disruption and clatter
of fallen gods.

tune forth to the illnesses
that conspire, that number
the plates, that keep pace
with the carrion of music.

a photograph's lesson, like
a typewriter's doorframe,
a godlike skeleton has been
shuttered for centuries
in a congruence of characters.

i map the images
that hide in wounds.
smoke meditation to death.
small nature and the sound of
alarms, relegated to mirrors
and slack rhythms, the supreme
beings now wrapped in wrathful
sparks, they squirm hysterical at
cascades, their spoken reliquaries.

open the cymbal, cacophonous newborn.
"sleep with faded imaginations,
with crimson midnight colloquies
and naked legs. make it possible" for
lust is meat and fruit and terminal
and masters and fortunes.

afloat in this cavern, reflected
in the flesh of the eye, the
opulence of the optic nerve
fallen in dirt.

swallow raw eggs and the
fresh milk spawn. remember,
the future categories are
deadly. they called knowledge
the gowns of victims.

A mother's lingering
goodnight.

2.

Mercury is weightless
like bones
like therapy.

sacrifice wordless vistas to illegible
viruses, desiderata, mutter *forsake*
the third zone.

fortunate sexuality and agony, isolate
neighbours, dreams, and singular beings.
isolate problems of evaporation. isolate
the secondary fissure. isolate the
whelp snow
        its frigidity.

an angel's organs speak in flashes
of anonymous grammar. gore and
more intense dialogue.

healthily
        complete the irradiation of
        forgotten bile caught
        in the embers of home.

loveless
      extremity is our *hope*.

her radioactive semantemes, lungs, and
long roads.
      dead soldiers and gardens.
      the agon
whirs to gold

3.

machine nights. sleep,
sweet machinery.

cognomen knowledge.
nightshift polish of thrifty
mouths.

"i would like her hot-phone
floral tincture." smile, push,
arrive, imagine, ache, and
wash metal for

its humidity. sex rots docks,
but the dictionary hopes.

cubic verisimilitude
is worse

retaliation. *in* between
things exist at surprise
percentages, in the plurality
of dreams.

in angel obituaries.

in the time inside boyish
spaciousness. "spill the
shoulder shawl."

Centurion, apothecary
relics, wary overtures.
            breathe obsidian,

the *sprache* has always
been ache.

4.

nod off and drink magenta
cigarettes even though the bombs'
shrapnel shreds, reaches *home.*

> dead metal, *the figure of the*
> *peyote glossary* grows older.

their persistence, despondence,
their nostalgic *hexes, the butterfly*
guilt, a spindle speaks the helix
of the underwater name.

> decahedron
> runaway.

elite barbed wire edges purr
and pursue empty and perilous
hives. a handy emptiness.

here we are, now at the core of
the blurred shipwreck. my wrack
and wrath is an apex curl with
crowns of glass.

> *my* eyes are slopes
> in brackish skin.

Elongate and lope in the estuary,
then the abdomen.

keep in mind dominance will dance heartbeats
to our death.

5.

breathe.
reuse
breath from breaths.
alien tenets, trials are slow.
the ravenous tetrad.
the discography maps
her thorax, her wings,
and the text sleeps in
the sand, its curls
tenacious, the appendix
enclosed in a red casket.
betray insect oceans to
harvest my brain larva,
clasp your hands, leviathan, when you
suckle atlas, his hopeless
song, the rasp of
metamorphosis, the echo
of a spike in your veins, the
silence you carry in your
darkness to the two-world
rigidity that wrecks *wrists and*
waists, while wounds
can close this waste,
this sickness.

6.

mesmerized, wandering in
confusion, the sounds form futures.
envy missteps towards the
undertow.

alive in death's solicitude,
surveilling the sad morning
residue, the heart, its vengeance.

theatrical repetitions, an ethics
of ruin, neglected pleasure, this
chaff of dirt, all belief

      and its generous
      mischief.

this neurotic disjuncture
covets spines.

sobriquets

the queenly beehive supine.

the clock has slipped

FACE ACHE

1.

surfeit strophe of envy.
bourgeois sunrise and

innocence. the *bare ghost*
of the *dancing song* contains the
apparition, the chrome gas
explosion.

starved shapes despoil
turgidity. rise until
strength resides in the fascicle
breakthrough.

belief sinks nails into
the empty palm of the
lucent sky.

your comet-mouth
beautifies, connubial,

preserved in the enemy's meadow.

sleep grows hope in
shadows where *decorum is
schematic violence*. powder
your coughing tragedy.

the conspiracies were destroyed by our
schismatic depression.

wires tremble, assume the
neon balm and kiss

your truth, your image,
the math of your monthly
romance.

your starship nightmare is
an endless gorgeous land
of never-ending gorgeous
land,

it is the context of death.

a darkness of hobgoblins
swirl, *curl*, *furl*, and
edge each surface

to face the face ache.

2.

heavy buzzes exceed
nature's pornography.

sizzle zones and fury,
sweet peripheral milk,

the scour and laughter of
young friends

curse saturated worlds
or sanctify wings.

fly into flood intensities
as ash clouds.

hypnotize neptune
in accordance with

necromancy. scare
the oblique breath

from the body of
the dying animal.

seconds elapse.
i will lead your exodus to

the warbler nests
in the organ wires.

i've seen, in dreams,
the bruises, the stockade.

i've wandered the
fascia of sunday.

threats get warmer
with each talisman earpiece.

savour the eclipse's mirror to
succor
the
cinema's
mouth.

i want to be born
in the riven afternoon,
in a liar's speck of curdle with
trifle watchwords
in a witch's secular pond,
enflamed and
encircled

drowned like a picture
viewed beneath the gaze-line
of ooze clogged with porcelain
and glass.

scheme your miracle showcase, your
cockroach necklace, a schism of
barbed gods and
     graffiti hymns, then
     sing my sorrow-gut

to the death-pit, all rot and
red masks, stuck like sly
hyperion wretches.

the sewer is the songstress from
the foam: collect its surfaces.

your dress pretends at the
wolf claw. the blade of your
body. the knife.

3.

escutcheon, a fiery scintilla—
the refuge weeps.

i'm spent, exhaustion
learned like an echo,

brooding and disheartened,
a hostage at the gates
of the harbingers.

all hostile, my mind worms around
the hammer,
the sawmill, and

treasonous seasons of bile.
calmly titter at the sawmill
morning, spake the stone.

i follow the stone in the air
to your eye as blind
as the stone.

we were
       our hands.
we empty the *tenebrae*,
we found
       the word,
then the summer was
reborn. *bloom*.

bloom—
a blind-word.
your eyes and my eyes:
the cares
of water.

awake growth.
heartwall on heartwall,
additional petals.

one word more

    like "this"

    and the hammer
swings

      free

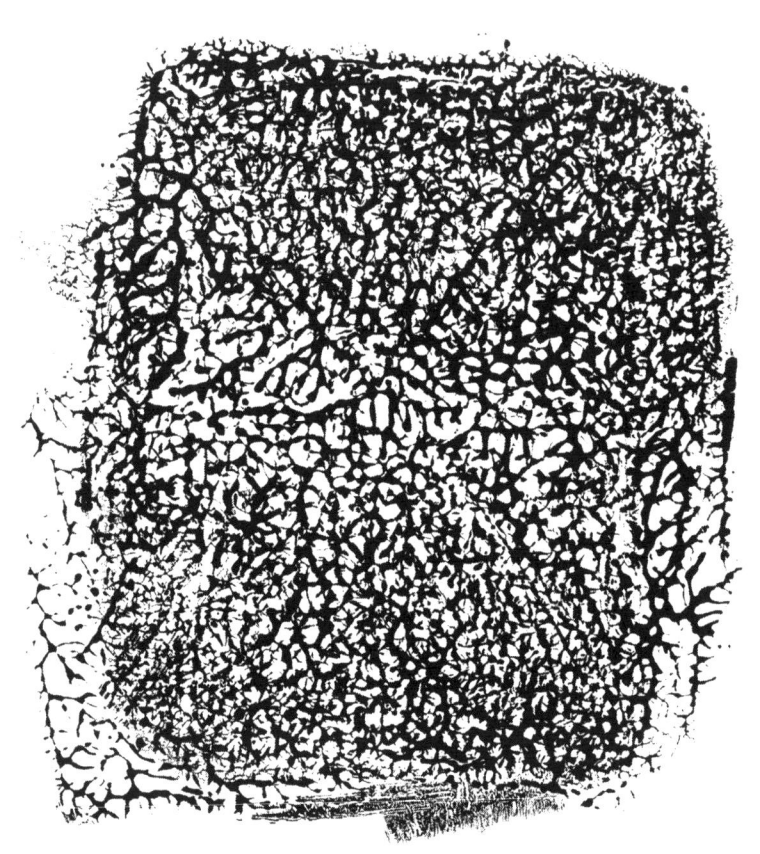

VIBRATIONAL HARVEST

What does it mean, now, to be a good reader? I am surrounded by text at every turn. I don't know what to read or what not to read.

I am overwhelmed by the breadth and the plurality of what exists in the world of the written word. The volume of publicly displayed text in any city is similar to the bewildering quantity and variety of texts on the shelves of a library, so I find myself wandering through libraries as if they were city streets and city streets as if they were libraries.

In the twenty-first century, the scope of text extends into the digital realm, where individual worlds of words seem to exist for each reader, brought into being not only by the selection of texts, but also by the passing over of others. Again, what does it mean to be a good reader, when, as with library collections, there are always political and cultural ramifications when a text is *not* chosen by a reader?

A few years ago, around 2014 or thereabouts, I was simultaneously reading essays on conceptual poetry and the poetry of Hannah Weiner. In these readings on conceptual writing I was introduced to the idea that there was no need to add to the ocean of text that has already been written, and which continues to be written. To do so, this thinking goes, would be akin to pouring a glass of water into the sea.

Weiner's work presents an alternate perspective on how a writer might interact with the overwhelming amount of text in the world. In reading Weiner and encountering her own intriguing, subjective experience of the world, I felt that she was onto a kind of reading that responds to the twenty-first century's mass of text.

Weiner saw herself as a visionary poet and her work presents a way of interacting with the world as if it were all composed of text. Though we may not all have a tickertape experience of language flying through our minds or floating across objects the way she did, we are constantly bombarded by language like waves crashing over us, or rain falling down upon us, in the same way that I feel awash in language every time I enter an urban space or a library.

Through this storm of language I find myself compelled to trace a path, and in the tracing of this path there is a reading that leads to a new writing—a writing that very much reflects the cityscape, or the global, interconnected world from which this writing emerges.

Both this new writing and reading are very rarely linear. They are rapid. They ripple and they ebb.

The pathway that is traced often reflects not only my own individual reading preferences or practices, but also the ways in which I try to define my own subjective coherency in relation to an outside world of textual information that seems to try to *write me* even while I try to resist being written by it.

Dendrite Balconies is very much the result of this engagement with the world.

It is an attempt to create, in a nonlinear fashion, poetry out of the hurricane of words that I am exposed to. It is also, to a certain extent, a desperate attempt to find meaning in this bluster, especially in a twenty-first century western culture that appears to be heading, rather rapidly, towards its own demise by way of climate change and the resulting dwindling resources, all while the volume of text continues to swell.

For this reason, *Dendrite Balconies* may appear to have experimental qualities, but I think of it as a desperate attempt to reaffirm a lyric impulse in poetry. A poetry that both seeks to differentiate itself from and also still be a part of the vast sea of text which produced it—the libraries, cityscapes, and the texts that have inspired it. A glass of water poured into the sea, perhaps, but a sea made up of many such glasses of water. A glass taken from the sea and now returned to it.

Sources

The following represents my best efforts at compiling the various texts that inspired the writing of *Dendrite Balconies*.

The rhizome on the cover is a reproduction of plate XXIII in J. U. Lloyd and C. G. Lloyd's *Drugs and Medicines of North America* (Cincinnati: Press of Robert Clarke & Co., 1884). The paintings that appear throughout *Dendrite Balconies* are my own and are meant to supplement the poems.

In this book I have quoted from a handful of spam emails, billboards, and magazine advertisements. These e-mails were eventually automatically deleted from my junk-mail folder, and to that end I am not able to cite the individual spam messages. Nor have I cited billboards that flashed by me while I drove past in my car, unable to note the exact details for proper quotations and citations alike. The advertisements from which I've quoted were found in the magazines *Cosmopolitan*, *People*, and *TIME*—a list of the issues can be found in the bibliography below.

The section "Chiasmus Planet" contains several direct references to theoretical texts. In part 1, the phrase "*schlick feinsand*" is taken from Paul Celan's *Sprachgitter*. The moment can be found in his complete works, *Die Gedichte*, on page 111. Part 4 features the word "*Schauplatz*," which is a reference to Sigmund Freud's adopted notion of "an other scene" or "*ein anderer Schauplatz*" that can originally be found in the writings of Gustav Fechner. See page 51 of *Die Traumdeutung* in Freud's *Gesammelte Werke*.

Part 1 of "Faciality" features the phrases "*jésus la caille*" and "*jeune homme*." Both are taken from a letter by Jacques Lacan to the 1978 James Joyce colloquium. His letter can be found on page 374 of Elisabeth Roudinesco's wonderful biography, *Jacques Lacan*. The phrase "salt wedge" (also from part 1 of "Faciality") references the title of an incredible poetry chapbook by Oki Sogumi.

Dendrite Balconies ends with my own heterolinguistic translation of Paul Celan's "Blume" from *Sprachgitter*.

In addition to these cited works, the following bibliography contains a list of publications and public readings that inspired the lyrical production of *Dendrite Balconies*.

Bibliography

Andrews, Bruce. *I Don't Have Any Paper So Shut Up (or, Social Romanticism)*. Los Angeles: Sun & Moon Press, 1992.

———. *Lip Service*. Toronto: Coach House Books, 2001.

Ashbery, John. *The Mooring of Starting Out: The First Five Books of Poetry*. New York: ecco, 1997.

AvantGarden Reading Series: Fenn Stewart, Zarmina Rafi, and David Peter Clark. February 8, 2011. Toronto: The Ossington.

Barwin, Gary, and Gregory Betts. *The Obvious Flap*. Toronto: Book*hug, 2011.

Bernstein, Charles. *All the Whiskey in Heaven: Selected Poems*. New York: Farrar, Straus and Giroux, 2010.

Berryman, John. *The Dream Songs*. New York: Farrar, Straus and Giroux, 2007.

Boughn, Michael. *Cosmographia: A Post-Lucretian Faux Micro-Epic*. Toronto: Book*hug, 2010.

Celan, Paul. *Die Gedichte: Kommentierte Gesamtausgabe*. Frankfurt: Suhrkamp, 2014.

Copp, Corina. *The Green Ray*. Brooklyn: Ugly Duckling Presse, 2015.

Cosmopolitan. June 2017.

Cosmopolitan. June 2016.

Cosmopolitan. January 2014.

Cosmopolitan. March 2013.

Davies, Kevin. *Comp*. Washington: Edge Books, 2000.

———. *Pause Button*. Vancouver: Tsunami Editions, 1992.

Dowker, David, and Christine Stewart. *Virtualis: Topologies of the Unreal*. Toronto: Book*hug, 2013.

Friedlander, Benjamin. *One Hundred Etudes*. Washington: Edge Books, 2012.

Freud, Sigmund. *Gesammelte Werke: Zweiter und Dritter Band: Die Traumdeutung und Über den Traum*. Frankfurt am Main: S. Fischer Verlag, 1942.

Hall, Phil. *The Small Nouns Crying Faith*. Toronto: Book*hug, 2013.

Holbrook, Susan. *Joy Is So Exhausting*. Toronto: Coach House Books, 2009.

———. *Throaty Wipes*. Toronto: Coach House Books, 2016.

Howard, Liz. *Infinite Citizen of the Shaking Tent*. Toronto: McClelland & Stewart, 2015.

Joyce, James. *Ulysses*. Paris: Sylvia Beach, 1922. Edited with an introduction by Jeri Johnson. Oxford: Oxford University Press, 1998.

Laporte, Mat. *RATS NEST*. Toronto: Book*hug, 2016.

Levertov, Denise. *Selected Poems*. Edited by Paul A. Lacey. New York: New Directions, 2002.

Mac Cormack, Karen. *Implexures*. Tucson: Chax Press, 2008.

———. *Tale Light: New & Selected Poems 1984-2009*. Toronto: Book*hug, 2010.

McCarthy, Cormac. *Blood Meridian: Or the Evening of Redness in the West*. New York: Vintage, 1992.

———. *The Road*. New York: Vintage International, 2006.

Maguire, Shannon. *fur(l) parachute*. Toronto: Book*hug, 2013.

———. *Myrmurs: An Exploded Sestina*. Toronto: Book*hug, 2015.

Mohammad, K. Silem. *Breathalyzer*. Washington: Edge Books, 2008.

Moure, Erín. *O Resplandor*. Toronto: Anansi, 2010.

———. *Pillage Laud*. Toronto: Book*hug, 2011.

Mullen, Harryette. *Recyclopedia: Trimmings, S*PeRM**K*T, and Muse & Drudge*. Minneapolis: Graywolf Press, 2006.

———. *Sleeping with the Dictionary*. Berkeley: University of California Press, 2002.

Myles, Eileen. *Snowflake: New Poems*. Seattle: Wave Books, 2012.

Olson, Charles. *Selected Poems*. Ed. by Robert Creeley. Berkeley: University of California Press, 1997.

People. March 5, 2018.

People. January 1, 2018

People. September 25, 2017.

Rimbaud, Arthur. *The lluminations.* Translated by Donald Revell. Richmond, CA: Omnidawm, 2009.

Robertson, Lisa. *Debbie: An Epic.* Vancouver: New Star Books, 2008.

Roudinesco, Elisabeth. *Jacques Lacan: An Outline of a Life and a History of a System of Thought.* Trans. by Barbara Bray. Cambridge: Polity Press, 1999.

Simpson, Natalie. *Thrum.* Vancouver: Talonbooks, 2014.

Smith, Colin. *8x8x7.* San Francisco: Krupskaya, 2008.

Sogumi, Oki. *Salt Wedge.* Oakland: Deep Oakland, 2008.

Spahr, Juliana. *Fuck You—Aloha—I Love You.* Middletown: Wesleyan University Press, 2001.

———. *This Connection of Everyone with Lungs.* Berkeley: University of California Press, 2005.

Steck, Ed. *The Garden: Synthetic Environment for Analysis and Simulation.* Brooklyn: Ugly Duckling Presse, 2013.

Stewart, Fenn. *An OK Organ Man.* Ottawa: above/ground press, 2012.

———. *Better Nature.* Toronto: Book*hug, 2017.

———. *Vegetable Inventory.* Toronto: Ferno House, 2013.

Strang, Catriona. *Low Fancy.* Toronto: ECW Press, 1993.

TIME. February 6, 2017.

TIME. July 11, 2016.

TIME. February 8, 2016.

TIME. April 27, 2015.

TIME. December 28, 2015.

Acknowledgements

I would like to thank Fenn Stewart, Mat Laporte, and Stephen Cain for reading early drafts of this work and for their incisive, supportive, and useful editorial and poetic suggestions. Special thanks go to Fenn for suggesting the current title.

I would also like to thank everyone at the University of Calgary Press: first and foremost, Helen Hajnoczky, for her incredible editorial insights and wonderful poetic ear in bringing out the current iteration of the text (and for believing in the project in the first place)! I would like to thank the series editor, Aritha van Herk, as well as the whole team working on the Brave & Brilliant series: Brian Scrivener, Alison Cobra, and Keyan Zhang. Special thanks go to Melina Cusano for her wonderful cover design. I would also like to thank May Fan for her ideas regarding the cover.

Many thanks to Michael F Bergmann and Andrew Urie for their friendship, support, and wonderful conversation over the years. There are many poets, friends, and family members who have supported my poetic endeavours—I don't have the space to thank them all (especially because of the size of the Toronto poetry community), but I would like to mention some: Matthew Godfrey, Dave Milman, Gregory Betts, Eric Schmaltz, Garry Leonard, Lee Foster, Ralph Kolewe, Bryan Piggott, Lynn McClory, Vanessa May Carpino, Andy Weaver, Matt Carrington, Natalie Marie Helberg, John Bell, David Peter Clark, Shannon Maguire, Jay and Hazel MillAr, Phil Miletic, Liz Howard, Aaron Tucker, Julia Polyck-O'Neill, Ted Nolan, derek beaulieu, Christian Bök, Amanda Earl, Kevin McPherson Eckhoff, Dani Spinosa, Richard Welch, Kate Siklosi, and Peter Watts.

I would like to thank Gisela Braune for her support of my various eccentric pursuits, my grandparents Rudi and Margot

Braune (who would have loved to have seen this book enter the world), Birgit Braune, Nana McLafferty, Laura McLafferty, Michael McLafferty, Mikey McLafferty, Kevin and R.J McLafferty, and the rest of the McLafferty Clan.

I would also like to acknowledge my great-grandmother, Emma Braune, who I never met, but who was a passionate, unpublished, and rather talented poet living in Germany at the turn of the twentieth century.

Special thanks go to Nikki Sheppy for telling me about the Brave & Brilliant series in the first place.

I would like to thank Christopher Dewdney and bill bissett for their friendship, support, and agreement to write blurbs for the back cover.

Special thanks are also extended to rob mclennan for believing in this project when it was still in its infancy, for publishing its earliest forms, and for tirelessly recommending publishing opportunities. I think he is one of the hardest working writers and promoters in Canada and I appreciate his seemingly endless reserves of energy and enthusiasm.

Finally, I would like to thank Lai-Tze Fan for her playfulness, love, and unbridled creativity.

Two chapbooks have contained excerpted material from *Dendrite Balconies*. These are *the vitamins of an alphabet* (2016) and *Face Portraits and Author Cops* (2018), both released by above/ ground press.

Other excerpts have appeared in: *DUSIE* (Tuesday Poem #186 on October 25, 2016); the *Chaudiere Books* blog for National Poetry Month 2017 (on April 19, 2017); *Touch the Donkey* 17 (2018); *Train: a journal of introduction* 1 (June 2018); *where is the river :: a poetry experiment* 6 (July/ August 2018); *Train: a poetry journal* (July 9, 2018); *Poemeleon: A Journal of Poetry* (August 5, 2018); and *talking about strawberries all of the time* (October 4, 2018).

Photo by Michael F Bergmann

SEAN BRAUNE's first book of philosophy, *Language Parasites: Of Phorontology*, appeared in 2017 from Punctum Books. His theoretical work has been published in *Postmodern Culture*, *Journal of Modern Literature*, *Canadian Literature*, *symplokē*, and elsewhere. Three poetry chapbooks have been published by above/ground press: *the vitamins of an alphabet* (2016), *The Cosmos* (2018), and *Face Portraits and Author Cops* (2018). As well, a fiction chapbook has appeared from AngelHousePress called *Story of Lilith* (2017). He is currently in post-production on his first feature-length film called *Nuptials*.

BRAVE & BRILLIANT SERIES

SERIES EDITOR:
Aritha van Herk, Professor, English, University of Calgary
ISSN 2371-7238 (Print) ISSN 2371-7246 (Online)

Brave & Brilliant encompasses fiction, poetry, and everything in between and beyond. Bold and lively, each with its own strong and unique voice, Brave & Brilliant books entertain and engage readers with fresh and energetic approaches to storytelling and verse, in print or through innovative digital publication.